D1609787

THE BOOK OF
PRACTICAL HOUSEHOLD
FORMULAS

THE BOOK OF
PRACTICAL HOUSEHOLD
FORMULAS

THORSONS PUBLISHERS LIMITED
Wellingborough, Northamptonshire

First published 1975
Second Enlarged Edition 1977

ISBN 0 7225 0313 X

PRINTED IN GREAT BRITAIN BY
LOWE AND BRYDONE (PRINTERS) LIMITED, THETFORD, NORFOLK

CONTENTS

PUBLISHER'S NOTE

While none of the mixtures in this book are any less safe than their commercial counterparts, and while care has been taken to avoid the inclusion of any dangerous constituents, they should nevertheless be treated with caution.

Always follow the golden rule, and keep your chemicals and mixtures in adequate, well-stopperéd and well-labelled containers from which the old labels have been removed. Also, keep all such items out of the reach of small children.

*   *   *

Note to US readers: The units used in this book are British weights and measures, together with their metric equivalents, and readers in America should bear in mind that the US gallon is only 5/6 of the British gallon.

INTRODUCTION

There is not much you cannot buy in the shops, and most of the time one is faced with a galaxy of alternative products, each manufacturer courting his potential customers with attractive packaging, aerosol dispensers, and loudly made claims of the particular efficacy of his particular piece of merchandise. In this there is perhaps no more competitive field than the household consumer market, and no one person more appealed to in expensive advertisements than Mrs Housewife.

Basic products, such as polishes, cleaners, stain removers, bleaches and disinfectants, all come in for the dramatic treatment and are given special colourings, odorizers and additives backed by a product name with impact, and extensive promotional activity. Such colourful competitiveness between the rival producers makes available to the housewife shelf-fulls of attractively packaged and easy-to-use 'convenience' products; but only at a price! After all, each time anyone buys such items she, or he, must bear a part of the cost of the multi-million pound advertising campaign, and the high cost of specially made and printed containers and cartons.

There is, of course, nothing wrong with all this—it makes for gaiety on the supermarket shelves, and fills the hoardings with colourful posters, and the TV 'natural breaks' with catchy jingles — but one must bear in mind that finally it is the consumer who foots the bill. So, if you are anxious to make some economies in your purchasing of day-to-day products (and who isn't?) then you have done the right thing in buying this book.

You will find in the following pages an extensive list of mixtures and methods for most of the everyday household products which can be easily made up in the home. You will not need any special equipment, and there are hints for improvisation, when this is called for, along with a guide to sources of supplies of raw materials. Also included are some less workaday handicraft formulas, and some mixtures for the more ambitious man or woman about the house, but basically the purpose of the book is to show how simply you can make up for yourself many of the items which you are probably at present paying dearly for.

Preparing the mixtures can be fun. It may take a little longer to produce the end result than buying in the shop, but you will have the satisfaction of self-sufficiency, and you should also be able to save yourself some money.

IMPROVISED APPARATUS

Most of the formulas in this book can be made up at home without the need for any special apparatus, and where it is necessary to use such things as 'water baths' and thermometers these can either be improvised from what you already have in the kitchen cupboard, or they can be bought quite cheaply. For instance, here are some ideas.

A makeshift 'water bath'
Use a large saucepan sufficient to hold a pudding basin and a quantity of water so that the basin floats.

The purpose of the 'water bath' is to permit the indirect heating of substances that it would be inadvisable to heat direct. The mixture to be heated should be put into the basin, and the saucepan put over direct heat so that as the temperature of the water rises it gently transmits its heat to the contents of the basin.

An improvised floating thermometer

In the preparation of some of the 'recipes' temperature is fairly critical and it is necessary to have some sort of thermometer. You may already have a jam-making or beer-making thermometer, or even a spare fish tank thermometer if you keep an aquarium. If not, they can be bought quite cheaply. On the other hand, if you have a small clinical type of thermometer this can be adapted by drilling out a hole through the centre of a wine bottle cork, and inserting the thermometer through the hole so that the bulb protrudes at the bottom and sufficient graduation shows at the top for you to check when the required temperature is reached. This can then be floated in a 'water bath' rather like a fishing float.

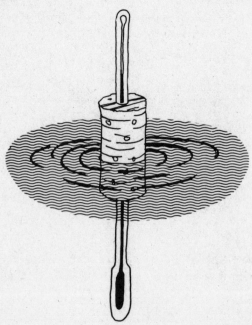

To crush crystals into powder

If a mixture calls for a chemical in powder form, but you find you only have it as crystals, there is no need to have to buy a pestle and mortar to crush them. You can do this just as effectively by putting the crystals to be crushed between two sheets of stout paper, and either 'rolling out' with a rolling pin, or crushing the crystals by rubbing over the paper with the bowl of a spoon.

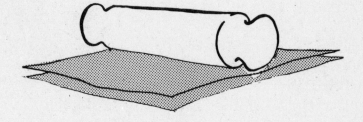

AROUND THE HOUSE

REMOVING STAINS FROM CARPETS

(i)   For the removal of grease spots and dirty marks on carpets the following can be quite effective.

Fuller's earth	4 oz. (115g)
White spirit	1 oz. (30g)
Potassium carbonate	8 oz. (225g)
Soft soap	

Mix the Fuller's Earth and potassium carbonate and soft soap shavings with the white spirit until a smooth paste is formed. Rub the paste into the grease spot or mark with a clean cloth, allow to dry and brush off.

(ii) Another way to remove new grease and oil marks is by rubbing dry flour well into the spot and allowing it to remain for some hours before brushing off. The idea is that the flour absorbs the grease, and that both are then removed by the brushing action.

(iii) Ink stains can be attacked by applying a thick layer of common salt which is then brushed off after leaving for a few minutes. Repeat the process until all the ink is absorbed and then wipe the carpet clean with lemon juice and warm water. This would only work immediately after the ink had been spilt.

(iv) As a simple cleaner for general stains use ordinary soap rubbed in with a damp flannel and rinse with dilute ammonia solution.

REMOVING STAINS FROM LEATHER

(i) Dab the oil spot carefully with a cloth soaked in spirits of sal ammoniac, leave to soak for a while and then wash the area with clean water. Repeat the process if necessary.

(ii) Oil spots can also be dealt with by applying with a clean sponge a mixture of warm water and vinegar. Petrol and benzene are also effective, but may cause some discoloration.

CLEANING WINDOWS

(i) For dealing with particularly dirty or greasy windows the addition of $\frac{1}{2}$ oz. (15g) washing soda per 2 pts. (1135ml) warm water will prove very effective. Equally as good is a tablespoonful of vinegar added to every 3 pts. (1705ml) warm water. Both these additives act as degreasants, making cleaning easier and leaving the windows with a sparkle. If using a wash leather it is best to use the vinegar method, for the leather's sake.

(ii) For internal use on windows, mirrors and any glass surface, the following mixture makes an ideal cleaner, but care should be taken with the ammonia, and it is advisable to wear rubber gloves when mixing.

Methylated spirit	$\frac{1}{4}$ pt. (140ml)
Ammonia solution (strong)	$\frac{1}{4}$ pt. (140ml)
Water	$\frac{1}{2}$ pt. (285ml)

Methylated spirit is, in fact, excellent for cleaning windows on its own, but the addition of ammonia enhances its action and gives it greater cleaning strength.

CLEANING MIRRORS

A method which is particularly effective for mirrors, and leaves them with a sparkle, is to rub the glass with a ball of soft paper dampened with methylated spirit, then sprinkle a little whiting on to a clean duster and rub the glass with it, and finally polish with clean dry paper or a wash leather.

TO PREVENT GLASS FROM MISTING UP

(i) Although this would not be able to cope with heavy condensation such as might occur on wash day, it can be quite effective in preventing a light formation of mist.

The method is to put a little calcium chloride on a glass dish and place on the window sill. The calcium chloride will absorb the moisture from the air near the window before it condenses on the glass and thus keeps the window clear. When saturated the calcium chloride may be dried and used again.

(ii) Apply a film of soap to the surface of the window or mirror by means of a damp cloth, then rub this off with a clean, dry cloth. This will prevent moisture settling on the surface of the glass.

GENERAL DEGREASANT

Soapy water is sometimes not enough when wiping down greasy surfaces, and the following is a useful ammonia-based degreasant for the more obstinate marks.

Strong ammonia solution	$1\frac{1}{2}$ fl. oz. (45ml)
Hard soap	$\frac{1}{2}$ lb. (225g)
Potassium nitrate	1 pinch

First of all cut the soap into shavings, dissolve in about $1\frac{1}{4}$ pt. (710ml) hot water and add a pinch of potassium nitrate. Allow to cool, strain through some muslin, and then mix in the ammonia solution. This can then be kept in a bottle, or bottles, ready for use.

FURNITURE POLISH

(i) A basic wax polish can be made from the following:

Beeswax	1 oz. (30g)
Turpentine	$\frac{1}{4}$ pt. (140ml)

Scrape the beeswax into shavings and leave these to dissolve in the turpentine. This is a slow process, and it may take a few days before all the wax is dissolved, but as soon as it is in solution give the bottle a shake and use in the normal way.

(ii) For the ambitious there is this more sophisticated formula. You will need some means of checking the temperature of the solution (a cooking thermometer will do, or a home brewer's or fish tank thermometer as long as it is graduated over 90°C – or *see page 12*).

Carnauba wax	$1\frac{1}{4}$ oz. (35g)
Beeswax	$\frac{1}{2}$ oz. (15g)
Paraffin wax	$\frac{1}{4}$ oz. (7g)
Stearic acid	1oz. (30g)
Triethanolamine	$\frac{5}{8}$ oz. (17g)
Naphtha	$\frac{3}{4}$ pt. (425ml)

Melt the carnauba wax, beeswax and paraffin wax together in a 'water bath' (*see page 11*), keeping the temperature of the water at 90°C. When melted, add the triethanolamine, and slowly pour in the naphtha, stirring all the time to maintain a clear solution. Next add $1\frac{1}{2}$ pt. (850ml) boiling water and stir briskly until the solution emulsifies. Remove from heat and stir gently until cool. The wax can then be spooned into a tin for use.

(iii) A simple, but very effective and economical polish can be made from:

Boiled linseed oil	$\frac{1}{2}$ pt. (140ml)
Vinegar	$\frac{1}{2}$ fl. oz. (15ml)

Mix well, use sparingly and leave to soak in before polishing.

FLOOR POLISH

Although not exactly cheap, the following mixtures produce good polish:

(i)
Carnauba wax	2 oz. (55g)
Beeswax	$\frac{1}{2}$ oz. (15g)
Turpentine	1 tablespoonful
Naphtha	1 pt. (570ml)

Using a 'water bath' (*see page 11*), melt the carnauba wax and beeswax together. Separately mix the turpentine and naphtha and add to the melted wax. Carry on heating until the mixture becomes clear and then allow to cool, stirring continuously. The polish can now be poured into a tin or jar ready for use.

(ii)
Carnauba wax	4 oz. (115g)
Stearic acid	$\frac{1}{2}$ oz. (15g)
Triethanolamine	$\frac{1}{4}$ oz. (7g)
Turpentine	$\frac{3}{8}$ pt. (215ml)

Melt the carnauba wax and stearic acid together in a 'water bath' (*see page 11*). Separately dissolve the triethanolamine in about a pint of water and heat almost to boiling. Now slowly pour in the melted wax and stearic acid, stirring all the time. Finally, stir in the turpentine, allow to cool and pour into a tin or jar ready for use.

(iii)	Carnauba wax	6 oz. (170g)
	Oleic acid	2 drops
	Triethanolamine	1 oz. (30g)
	Borax	$\frac{1}{4}$ oz. (7g)

Melt the carnauba wax in a 'water bath' (*see page 11*), and add two drops of oleic acid (this acts as an emulsifier). Now add the triethanolamine slowly, stirring all the time. Separately boil a pint (570ml) of water and dissolve the borax in it, and stir the solution into the mixture in the 'water bath' until clear. Now slowly add a further $1\frac{1}{2}$ pt. (850ml) of boiling water, still stirring all the time. When thoroughly mixed allow to cool and store in a tin or jar.

PIANO KEY BLEACHER

The ivory keys of old pianos tend to go an unsightly yellow, and these can be restored to something like their original condition by first wiping the keys with warm washing soda solution to remove the grime. Then sponge down with clean water and allow to dry. Next wipe the keys with ammonia solution, followed by a further wipe with hydrogen peroxide. Finally wash off with clean water.

Note: Take care to use rubber gloves throughout.

REMOVING 'HEAT' RINGS FROM TABLES

Those nasty white rings that remain on the table top when someone has stood a hot or wet cup on the surface can be taken out by using a half-and-half mixture of cooking oil and salt. Rub the mixture on the ring, leave for about an hour and then rub off.

LEATHER POLISH

Similar in ingredients to one of the floor polishes, but different in consistency, is the following which is specially for polishing leather. A thermometer will again be needed with this one (*see page 12*).

Stearic acid	$1\frac{1}{2}$ oz. (45g)
Triethanolamine	$\frac{1}{8}$ oz. ($3\frac{1}{2}$g)
Carnauba wax	$\frac{3}{4}$ oz. (21g)
Turpentine	$\frac{1}{8}$ pt. (70ml)

Dissolve the stearic acid and triethanolamine in water and boil. Separately, melt the carnauba wax in the turpentine by heating in a 'water bath' (*see page 11*), and when this mixture has reached a temperature of 90°C combine the two solutions, remove from heat, and stir until cold.

SHOE POLISH

A polish suitable for shoes and boots.

Soap flakes	1 oz. (30g)
Potassium carbonate	$\frac{1}{2}$ oz. (15g)
Beeswax	5 oz. (140g)

Slice up the beeswax and add to a pint of water. Stir in the soap flakes and potassium carbonate, and boil the solution until a smooth paste is formed.

To stiffen the paste, separately mix:

Gum arabic powder	$\frac{1}{2}$ oz. (15g)
Icing sugar	$1\frac{1}{2}$ oz. (45g)

and add while the mixture is still hot.

For black polish, include 10 oz. (280g) of charcoal powder with the gum arabic and sugar.

24

CLEANSERS, DEODORIZERS, DISINFECTANTS AND BLEACHES

Cleansing Powder

Cleansing powder for the W.C. can be mixed from:

Slaked lime (fine powder)	11¼ oz. (320g)
Carbolic acid powder	1 oz. (30g)

Combine the two powders, sieve if necessary, and store in an air tight tin ready for use.

W.C. deodorizer

An effective, although not exactly cheap deodorizer, can be prepared for the toilet from the following:

Ferric chloride	½ oz. (15g)
Zinc chloride	½ oz. (15g)
Aluminium chloride	½ oz. (15g)
Calcium chloride	½ oz. (15g)
Magnesium chloride	¼ oz. (7g)

Mix all the items thoroughly together and, if to be used in powder form, leave in an open tin in a suitable place in the toilet out of reach of children.

Alternatively, the combined powders can be dissolved in ⅓ pt (200ml) of water. If a solution is used a sufficient quantity will have to be poured into a saucer for it to do its deodorizing work, or you may be able to make up an absorbent 'wick' device with a piece of absorbent felt and a suitable bottle.

General disinfectant

For an all-purpose domestic disinfectant mix these ingredients together thoroughly:

Camphor powder	1 oz. (30g)
Carbolic acid	12 oz. (340g)
Ammonia	¾ fl. oz. (21ml)
Water	½ fl. oz. (15ml)

When mixed store in a bottle. Can be used for sinks, drains and toilets, either neat or diluted with water.

Household bleach

If you can obtain some chlorinated lime, a useful bleach can be made up as under:

Chlorinated lime	2 oz. (55g)
Washing soda	3 oz. (85g)

Mix the lime and soda together and stir into 1 pt. (570ml) of water and leave to stand for a few days. Filter the solution through some muslin before use. Good for W.C.'s, sinks and obstinate stains. Dilute accordingly.

TO REMOVE WAX AND GREASE FROM FABRIC

An effective method is to lay the material with the grease spot on top of a sheet of blotting paper and to apply a warm iron to the spot. The heat from the iron melts the grease and the absorbent blotting paper then soaks it up, leaving the fabric free.

METAL POLISHES AND CLEANERS

Here are some ideas for make-it-yourself metal polishes and cleaners:

Brass

Vinegar	$\frac{1}{4}$ oz. (7g)
Salt	$\frac{1}{4}$ oz. (7g)
Tripoli	$\frac{1}{4}$ oz. (7g)
Olive oil	$\frac{1}{4}$ oz. (7g)

Rub the brass with a mixture of vinegar and salt, and wipe off immediately with warm water. Polish with tripoli and olive oil.

Copper

Iron oxide	1 oz. (30g)
Ground pumice stone	3 oz. (85g)
Oleic acid	

Mix together the iron oxide and pumice and add sufficient oleic acid to form a paste. Apply this to the surface with a linen pad, taking care to avoid scratching when rubbing, and wipe off with a clean, dry cloth.

Gilt

(i) Add about 5 drops of dilute ammonia solution to a cupful of industrial methylated spirit and brush the mixture over the surface of the item to be cleaned. If it is necessary to rub it in take care to be very gentle. Leave for a few minutes and then brush over the surface again, using a clean soft brush dipped in water and leave the article to dry.

(ii) Another method is to dissolve some alum in boiling water and either immerse the article to be cleaned in the solution or apply the solution to the article with a cloth. The amount of alum to be used depends on how dirty the object is, but it is best to begin by using very little and increasing the strength of the solution if necessary. When clean the article can be dried with a clean cloth.

Silver

| (i) | Levigated chalk | 1 oz. (30g) |
| | Sodium thiosulphate | 1 oz. (30g) |

Make a paste of the chalk and sodium thiosulphate mixed with a little water, and apply this to the silverware with a soft brush. Rub well and rinse in clean water, or leave the paste to dry and rub off with a clean cloth.

(ii) For only slightly tarnished articles the following mixture is quite adequate.

| Chalk | 3 oz. (85g) |
| Soap flakes | 1 oz. (30g) |

Mix the soap flakes and chalk and add water until a thin paste is formed. Rub this paste on to the silverware, and polish until clean.

(iii) Another method, which does not involve polishing, is to dissolve washing soda in boiling water in the proportions of half a cupful to every $1\frac{1}{2}$ pints, and to put the article in the solution and drop in a few milk bottle tops. When clean take out the article, rinse and dry.

Stainless Steel

There is no better way of cleaning stainless steel than by the use of a damp cloth and a little soft soap. A rubbing action will remove all grease, and if the surface is then gone over with a dry cloth, it will leave it shining bright.

CHINA CEMENT

No matter how careful you are, sooner or later an accident will happen and someone will drop a treasured ornament or a cup from your best tea service, and you will gaze in despair at the broken pieces on the floor. There is hope of patching up the damage, though, and if the article is not too shattered the following cement will do the trick.

Gum arabic	$\frac{1}{2}$ oz. (15g)
Plaster of paris	a packet
Water (boiling)	$\frac{1}{4}$ pt. (140ml)

Slowly dissolve the gum arabic in the boiling water by adding gradually and stirring all the time. Now add sufficient plaster of paris to form a thick paste. Apply this paste to the broken edges of the china with a brush and press the parts together with a firm and steady pressure. If necessary, use tape to hold the pieces in place while drying. When dry the join or joins will be invisible.

ANTI-MOTH MIXTURE

Here is a spicey mixture, the aromatic effect of which serves to keep moths at bay.

Cloves	$\frac{1}{2}$ oz. (15g)
Caraway seeds	$\frac{1}{2}$ oz. (15g)
Nutmeg	$\frac{1}{2}$ oz. (15g)
Mace	$\frac{1}{2}$ oz. (15g)
Cinnamon	$\frac{1}{2}$ oz. (15g)
Orris root	$2\frac{1}{2}$ oz.(70g)

Grind all the above together and put the powder into fabric sachets – rather like 'lavender bags' – and hang them in your clothes cupboard.

OVEN CLEANER

(i) A strong solution of caustic soda can be used for this onerous task, but great care should be taken in handling the liquid, and rubber gloves should be worn at all times when using it as it can cause burns if it comes into contact with the skin. Make up the solution, using 1 oz. (30g) of caustic soda to 1 pt. (570ml) of water and apply to the walls of the oven (preferably pre-heated) with an old paint brush. Finally wipe down with clean warm water.

(ii) Another strong degreasant suitable for ovens can be mixed from the following:

Methylated spirit	$\frac{1}{2}$ pt. (285ml)
Ammonia solution (strong)	$\frac{1}{2}$ pt. (285ml)
Water	$\frac{1}{2}$ pt. (285ml)

Stir together thoroughly and put into well capped battles immediately after mixing. Care should be taken when handling the solution, and rubber gloves are advised. Especial care should also be taken if using this in an oven with a pilot light as the methylated spirit is inflammable.

HOUSEHOLD AMMONIA

An ammonia based solution can be made up ready for a variety of cleaning jobs from:

Oleic acid	1 fl. oz. (30ml)
Methylated spirit	1 fl. oz. (30ml)
Ammonia solution (strong)	$\frac{1}{3}$ pt. (200ml)
Water	1 pt. (570ml)

Pour the acid into a bottle; separately mix the methylated spirit and ammonia with the water, and pour this into the bottle with the acid. Cork tightly and allow to stand for a week before use.

REMOVING STAINS FROM GLASS BOTTLES

(i) Make a strong solution of washing soda and warm water, add a little lime, and leave in the bottle to soak.

(ii) Less obstinate stains should yield to a mixture of vinegar and water.

TO LOOSEN GLASS STOPPERS

Quite often glass stoppers in decanters and bottles get firmly stuck and resist all efforts to twist and pull them free. There is an instance when brute force is of little use and could indeed result in a breakage, so apply some warm salad oil around the stopper so that it seeps down into the neck of the bottle. Leave for a while, then tap the stopper gently with a piece of wood and it should come free.

FLY CATCHERS

Both fly sprays and vapour devices are very effective but the big problem is that they load the air with toxic particles which settle on everything in sight and consequently are not really suitable for use in the kitchen, which usually is just where the fly problem can be at its worst.

So, although somewhat unsightly, the old-fashioned fly paper is hard to beat. To make these at home you will need some strips of stout brown paper about 2 inches wide and stiffened by dipping into some size. These strips will form the bases onto which you can spread the mixture you find most effective in attracting the flies and causing them to stick to the surface. Here are three to try:

(i) Rosin powder   2oz. (55g)
      Raw linseed oil $\frac{1}{2}$ oz. (15g)
      Honey $\frac{1}{2}$ oz. (15g)

Melt the rosin and raw linseed oil together in a small saucepan and mix in the honey. When mixed together spread liberally over both sides of the sized strip of brown paper, attach a 'bulldog' clip to each end of the strip (this facilitates hanging, and also serves to 'weight' the bottom end).

(ii) Castor oil   2 oz. (55g)
       Rosin powder $4\frac{1}{2}$ oz. (130g)

Melt the ingredients together in a small saucepan and spread onto a paper strip. Hang as above.

(iii) Cobalt chloride $\frac{1}{4}$ oz. (7g)
       Brown sugar   1 oz. (30g)

Dissolve the cobalt chloride in $\frac{3}{4}$ pt. (425ml) of hot water and add the sugar. Instead of using the sized strip of brown paper, this time saturate some absorbent paper with the solution and hang in the same way as above.

PUTTING OUT SMALL FIRES

If prompt action is taken small fires can be extinguished before they get out of hand, but there is one very important rule to bear in mind: NEVER USE A LIQUID EXTINGUISHER ON ELECTRICALLY CAUSED FIRES, OR ON BURNING OIL!

Dry Extinguisher

The most likely place for a fire to begin is in the kitchen and it is very wise to keep something standing by in case of emergency. There is perhaps little better than a bucket of sand for this purpose, although an effective alternative is ordinary baking soda. Also the following mixture can be kept standing by in a large glass jar:

Common salt	3 oz. (85g)
Baking soda	4 oz. (115g)
Ammonium chloride	3 oz. (85g)

Such dry powder extinguishers are quite safe to use on electrical fires and burning oil, and would be of particular use in putting out the flames when cooking oil catches light.

Liquid extinguisher

The obvious liquid fire extinguisher is, of course, water; and for special solutions to be of any acceptable use they need to be in pressurized containers with directional nozzles. Such fire-fighting appliances can be bought and kept in suitable places, or as an alternative buckets of water and a stirrup pump are an adequate method of fighting an outbreak of fire. It should be remembered, though, that this would not do for electrically caused fires (such as a burning TV) or oil fires (such as a flaming deep-fryer).

Naturally, if anything shows the slightest sign of getting out of hand the fire brigade should be summoned instantly.

FIREPROOFING

Apart from cooking fires, another danger in the kitchen can lie in the use of polystyrene ceiling tiles. Flame-proof versions of such tiles can now be bought, but if inflammable tiles are used there is a real risk of them catching light above the cooker.

Polystyrene ceiling tiles
A fire-proofing solution for the ceiling tiles can be made up from the following:

Boric acid	$7\frac{1}{2}$ oz. (210g)
Sodium phosphate	5 oz. (140g)

Dissolve the chemicals in about 4 pt. (2270ml) of water, and apply to the tiles with a paint brush: or if the tiles are not yet in position, by dipping each tile in the solution. It is advisable, before starting, to experiment with the solution over a small area, as it may affect the colouring of the tiles.

Alternative mixtures which can be used in the same way are:

(a)	Borax	5 oz. (140g)
	Boric acid	4 oz. (115g)
(b)	Ammonium sulphate	8 oz. (225g)
	Boric acid	3 oz. (85g)
	Borax	2 oz. (55g)

Mixture (b) should be heated to about 50°C before applying.

36

Textiles

Good fire-proofing solutions for canvas and other such material can be mixed from the following:

(i)
Ferrous sulphate	1 oz. (30g)
Epsom salts	1 oz. (30g)
Ammonium chloride	1 oz. (30g)
Ammonia alum	3 oz. (85g)
Starch	

Mix the ferrous sulphate, epsom salts and ammonium chloride together, then add the ammonia alum, and stir in until the mixture has a paste-like consistency. Dry the paste out using a low heat, and when making up the solution for treating the fabric to be fire-proofed add one part of the final mixture to two parts of starch dissolved in water. The solution can either be painted on or the fabric can be dipped in the solution.

(ii)
Ammonium sulphate	4 oz. (115g)
Ammonium carbonate	1¼ oz. (35g)
Borax	1 oz. (30g)
Boric acid	1½ oz. (45g)
Starch	1 oz. (30g)

Dissolve the ingredients in 2½ pt. (1420ml) of water and heat to 30°C. Saturate the fabric by dipping it into the solution and then allow to dry. This solution is particularly useful for lightly-woven fabrics.

Wood

Wood cannot be made completely fire-proof, but the following — although a lengthy process — is quite effective. Wood so treated is said to be incombustible even when great heat is applied.

Manganese chloride	$3\frac{1}{4}$ oz. (90g)
Orthophosphoric acid	2 oz. (55g)
Magnesium carbonate	$1\frac{1}{4}$ oz. (35g)
Boric acid	1 oz. (30g)
Ammonium chloride	$2\frac{1}{2}$ oz. (70g)

Mix all the ingredients together and dissolve in about 5 pt. (2840ml) of water. Boil the solution, immerse the wooden item to be treated, and keep boiling for six to eight hours.

Another less elaborate process is to 'paint' on with a brush the following chemicals dissolved in about $1\frac{1}{4}$ pt. (710ml) of water.

Potassium carbonate	$2\frac{1}{2}$ oz. to 5 oz. (70g to 140g)
Ammonium borate	1 oz. to 2 oz. (30g to 55g)

The resistance to flame of wood treated in this way is greatly enhanced.

38

REMOVING STAINS FROM CLOTHES

Here are some mixtures and methods for dealing with those awkward stains and marks which normal washing won't shift.

Grease Stains

(i)	Saponine	$\frac{1}{2}$ teaspoonful
	Industrial methylated spirit	$\frac{1}{2}$ oz. (15g)
	Benzene	$\frac{1}{2}$ pt. (285ml)

Mix all three well together and keep in a well stoppered bottle and apply with a cloth when using.

(ii) Benzene by itself is effective, and white spirit or carbon tetrachloride will also shift some stains. After treatment it is a good idea to wash the garment in warm soapy water with a little household ammonia added.

Ink Stains
(i) Soak a piece of blotting paper in a concentrated solution of oxalic acid and allow it to dry. Now, lay the blotting paper directly over the ink stain, and it will usually remove the ink from the fabric completely. Care should be taken with oxalic acid since it can remove the colour from some fabrics.

(ii) For particularly stubborn stains, dip the garment in boiling water and rub the stain with oxalic acid crystals. Next, soak in a solution of 1 oz. (30g) chlorate of lime to 2 pt. (1135ml) of water, and finally rinse thoroughly in clean warm water. Again, the oxalic acid should be used with caution as it can remove the colour. It is best to experiment with a small unimportant area first.

| (iii) | Cream of tartar | 1 oz. (30g) |
| | Citric acid powder | 1 oz. (30g) |

Mix the two powders together ready for use. Take the garment and lay the stained part on a hot plate and moisten with hot water. Now rub in the powder with the bowl of a spoon until the stain disappears. Finally rinse out the garment in clean water.

Ball-point pen stain

Stains from ball-point pens are generally very obstinate, and are often impossible to remove, but here is something to try.

First of all, before doing anything else, rub soap into the stain. Now wipe off with a damp cloth, and repeat the sequence. Finally, attack the remains of the stain with a solvent such as benzene.

Paint stains

(i) Before the paint has dried it can be removed by liberal application of turpentine or benzene. The best method is to hold an absorbent pad beneath the stain, so that the paint will soak through into the pad.

(ii) If the paint has dried there is little that can be done. However, soaking the garment in ammonia solution may remove it, or failing this the stained area can be soaked in a 2 to 1 mixture of ammonia and white spirit. Care should be taken as prolonged soaking in such solutions might weaken the fibres, and these methods should be regarded as a last resort.

(iii) Emulsion paint presents no problem while it is still wet, but is very difficult to remove after it has dried so the rule here is to soak the garment without delay after it has been splashed with paint.

DECORATING

CLEANING PAINT BRUSHES

It goes without saying that if you keep your brushes clean they will last longer and give better service. Emulsion paint presents very little problem since it is only necessary to rinse under a tap after use. A bit more trouble has to be taken with other paints, but it is well worth it.

A good tip first of all is to remove the 'weight' of paint in the brush by resting the brush on an old newspaper and running the back of a knife blade down the bristles to 'press out' the paint. Turn the brush over and repeat the process. Then run the brush over a piece of waste wood.

Now the remaining paint can be washed out with solvent as follows:

Type of Paint	Solvent
Cellulose	Amyl acetate, mixed for cheapness with wood naphtha
Oil	Paraffin or white spirit
Polyurethane	Paraffin or white spirit
Rubber	Petrol
Spirit varnish	Methylated spirit
Washable distemper	Weak solution of vinegar

Finally, wash the brush out in warm soapy water and leave to dry. Put an elastic band round the bristles if they stick out. All this should be done immediately after the painting job is finished, since if the brush is left it becomes increasingly difficult to clean.

44

CLEANING DOWN PAINTWORK

For this there is little better than a bucket of warm water and a cupful of washing soda. Use a sponge to wipe the paintwork — wearing rubber gloves — and rinse off with clean warm water.

PUTTY

(i) For a simple putty mix some whiting with sufficient linseed oil to turn it into a dough-like consistency.

(ii) For something more elaborate mix together whiting, powdered white lead and zinc oxide, and add linseed oil to bind. Knead the ingredients, adding more linseed oil if necessary.

(iii) A waterproof putty can be made from:

Red lead	5 oz. (140g)
White lead	5 oz. (140g)
China clay	4 oz. (115g)
Linseed oil	

Mix the red lead, white lead and clay and add linseed oil until the mixture becomes kneadable. This is particularly good for sealing gas pipes and water pipes.

Care should be taken when using lead compounds, and the product should not be accessible to children.

PUTTY SUBSTITUTE

Boil 1 lb. (455g) of flour in 6 pt. (3410ml) of water, and add a teaspoonful of alum. Soak torn up pieces of newspaper in this paste until a putty-like consistency is obtained. This is particularly useful for fllling cracks and holes in woodwork prior to painting.

PUTTY SOFTENER

To remove putty which has set hard, apply paraffin oil. This dissolves the linseed oil in the putty, and quickly penetrates throughout.

VARNISH FOR FLOORS

As a basic varnish for floors dissolve about 10 oz. (285g) of shellac in $2\frac{1}{2}$ pt. (1420ml) of industrial methylated spirit.

KNOT SEALER

With most timber being unseasoned these days knots are inclined to ooze resin, especially if subjected to the sunshine. To seal off such 'leaking' knots use:

Shellac	5 oz. (140g)
Sandarac	1 oz. (30g)
Industrial methylated spirit	1 pt. (570ml)

Dissolve the shellac and sandarac in the methylated spirit and strain before applying by brush to the offending knots.

CLEAR VARNISH

A quick-drying clear varnish can be made up by dissolving scraps of 'expanded polystyrene' in amyl acetate. Care should be taken with this, however, since the acetate is highly inflammable and very pungent.

WHITEWASH

Although emulsion paint has generally taken its place, good old-fashioned whitewash is a lot cheaper if not so convenient to use. You can make it up with ordinary whiting, size, a little blue colouring matter and water.

WALLPAPER PASTES

Here are three formulas for wallpaper paste:

(i)   Rye flour   1 lb (455g)
        Pulverized colophony $\frac{1}{2}$ oz. (15g)

Mix the rye flour in 1 pt. (570ml) cold water until all lumps have dissolved. Add this mixture to 3 pt. (1700ml) boiling water, and simmer if necessary to thicken the paste. While still hot, stir in the pulverized colophony a little at a time.

   If the paste is too thick, thin with a little hot water – never cold water. This paste is extremely strong and is suitable for use on heavy wallpaper.

(ii)   Wheat flour   2 lb. (905g)
        Alum   1 oz. (30g)

Stir the wheat flour into $1\frac{3}{4}$ pt. (995ml) cold water until a lump-free mixture is formed. Separately, dissolve the alum in $\frac{1}{4}$ pt. (140ml) hot water. Now combine the wheat flour mixture with $4\frac{3}{4}$ pt. (2700ml) boiling water, stirring well, and boil again if necessary to thicken the paste. Finally, stir in the alum solution.

(iii)	Starch	4 oz. (115g)
	White dextrine	2 oz. (55g)
	Borax	1 oz. (30g)
	Glycerine	3 fl. oz. (85ml)

Mix together thoroughly the starch, dextrine and $\frac{1}{2}$ pt. (285ml) of cold water. Separately, dissolve the borax in $3\frac{1}{4}$ pt. (1845ml) of boiling water and add the glycerine. Pour the first mixture into the second, stirring until the combined solution becomes translucent.

This paste remains pliable after use, and so is particularly useful for materials where flexibility is required.

WALLPAPER REMOVER

The object of any method of removing wallpaper is to soften the paste. This can usually be achieved simply by brushing on liberal applications of cold or tepid water until the paper is thoroughly soaked. The paper can then either be pulled or scraped off.

If this method is not entirely satisfactory, a little baking soda may be added to the water before soaking the paper.

After the removal of the paper, the wall should be washed with clean water.

WALLPAPER CLEANER

This is more a tip than a formula, but nevertheless useful to know since it is an effective method for cleaning up dirty wallpaper. The simple 'trick' is to use stale bread cut into thick slices, and to wipe down the walls lightly with the 'flat' of the slice. This works rather like a pencil rubber does; and when finished all you have to do is sweep up the crumbs.

WALL WATERPROOFER

For internal use

Dissolve $1\frac{1}{4}$ lb (680g) calcium chloride in $\frac{1}{2}$ gallon (2275ml) of water. Mix together equal parts of a concentrated solution of sodium silicate and water. Apply the first solution to the wall and follow this by an application of the second solution. Repeat the sodium silicate solution coating if drying of the damp wall does not occur.

To prevent discoloration of any subsequent wallpaper, a coat of cheap varnish should be applied to the prepared wall.

For external brickwork

Soap	12 oz. (340g)
Alum	4 oz. (115g)

Dissolve the soap in 1 gallon (4545ml) of boiling water and brush the hot solution liberally over the outside surface of the wall. Allow to dry for twenty-four hours. Dissolve the alum in 2 gallons (9090ml) of cold water and apply over the coatings of the soap solution. Two or three applications may be necessary for completely satisfactory results. The operations should not be carried out if there is any likelihood of rain before the process is complete.

PLASTIC WOOD

An effective wood substitute can be made for 'filling' purposes from the following ingredients (quantities according to requirements):

Glue
Tissue paper
Linseed oil
Chalk

Boil up the glue, and when melted add the tissue paper, which will readily go to pieces. Add linseed oil, and finally stir in the chalk until the required consistency is reached. The mass should form a thick, kneadable dough which can be used for filling cracks and holes in woodwork. The mixture will set hard in two or three days.

NATURAL-WOOD FINISH

To obtain a fine natural-wood finish on such surfaces as plywood door panels and other wood fittings, paint with a mixture of three parts white spirit to one part polyurethane varnish. Rub down with fine sandpaper, apply a second coat consisting of one part white spirit to one part varnish, and rub down again. The result is a natural smooth semi-matt finish, resistant to dirt and household stains.

Note: The surface must be clean or cleaned to the required appearance before application of the varnish to obtain that lasting 'new look'.

MEDICAL

SPECIAL WARNING

Any unusual symptom, however trivial it may seem to be, should be reported to a doctor without delay. Self-diagnosis by the layman can sometimes have serious consequences, and it is not without good reason that most of the drugs used in doctors' prescriptions are not available to the general public.

Nevertheless, there are a few formulas for minor ailments which can usefully be mixed at home, and these are reproduced here with the proviso that medical attention should be sought if any symptoms do not clear up within a reasonable period.

MINOR BURN REMEDY

Here is something to alleviate the discomfort of a minor burn, but it should be understood that the remedy is only for very minor burns, and that anything more serious should be attended to by a doctor.

You will need some castor oil and one or two eggs. Break the eggs and separate the whites, add half a cupful of castor oil and beat into a thick creamy paste. Apply this paste to the burn, repeating frequently to prevent the surface becoming dry or sticky, and leave uncovered.

TO MAKE CASTOR OIL DRINKABLE

If for any reason castor oil has to be administered it can be made more palatable in the following way:

Castor oil	$1\frac{1}{2}$ oz. (45g)
Powdered gum arabic	$\frac{1}{4}$ oz. (7g)
Sugar	$\frac{1}{4}$ oz. (7g)
Peppermint water	$\frac{1}{2}$ oz. (15g)

Grind the sugar and the gum arabic together, and add the oil, mixing thoroughly. Add the peppermint water little by little, whisking well until an emulsion is formed. It is now ready for taking.

COUGH SWEETS

This recipe is not really a money-saver and unless you enjoy
doing things yourself it would be better to buy such sweets from
the shop.

Sugar	1 lb. (455g)
Tartaric acid	1 teaspoonful
Oil of anise	$\frac{1}{4}$ teaspoonful
Oil of peppermint	2 to 3 drops
Water	7 fl. oz. (200ml)

Thoroughly mix the ingredients and bake in a shallow tray in a
hot oven. Remove when the mixture has set and break into small
pieces.

INSECT REPELLENTS

If you are going camping, here are two mixtures for keeping insects at bay.

(i) Mix the following together and apply to the exposed skin:

Oil of cassia	1 oz. (30g)
Oil of camphor	2 oz. (55g)
Olive oil	3 oz. (85g)

(ii) This one is quite potent, and should perhaps only be used in dire circumstances, as it can be 'human repellent' as well!

Dimethyl phthalate	1 oz. (30g)
Industrial methylated spirit	1 oz. (30g)
Lavender water	

Mix the dimethyl phthalate and industrial 'meths' and add a few drops of lavender water to 'sweeten'.

(iii) Mosquito powder

Eucalyptus oil	$\frac{1}{4}$ oz. (7g)
Powdered talc (sterilized)	$\frac{1}{2}$ oz. (15g)
Powdered starch	$3\frac{1}{2}$ oz.(100g)

Mix well and rub into the exposed areas of skin.

INSECT STING LOTION

If all has failed and the insect has penetrated your defences and delivered its sting, the resulting discomfort can be alleviated by applying to the 'bite' a solution of 1 oz. (30g) baking soda and about $\frac{1}{2}$ pt. (285ml) water, adding a drop or two of perfume if preferred.

For wasp stings a dab with vinegar is very effective, and bee stings can be eased with a dilute solution of ammonia or just by rubbing with a moist cake of soap.

DR EPSOM'S SOLUTION

Used externally, Epsom salts can solve a lot of spotty problems. This solution deep cleanses the pores, removing all impurities.

Epsom salts (fine)	$\frac{1}{4}$ oz. (7g)
Water (boiled)	$\frac{1}{2}$ pt. (285ml)
Borax (powdered)	$\frac{1}{4}$ oz. (7g)

Dissolve the Epsom salts in the water, and bathe the face (or spotty area) with the solution using gauze swabs or cotton wool dabs. This must be done twice a day, morning and night, for at least a week. Use a fresh solution each time and, of course, a fresh piece of gauze or cotton wool. When it has dried in, wash in hot water to which you have added the borax. Dry thoroughly, preferably by dabbing skin with a towel. Keep the salty solution away from your eyes.

DENTURE CLEANER

Here are two non-effervescent mixtures for cleaning dentures.

(i)	Sodium perborate	2 oz. (55g)
	Common salt	$1\frac{1}{2}$ oz. (45g)
	Trisodium phosphate	$1\frac{1}{2}$ oz. (45g)

Mix thoroughly and flavour with one or two drops of oil of cloves or oil of peppermint.

(ii)	Sodium percarbonate	2 oz. (55g)
	Common salt	2 oz. (55g)
	Washing soda	1 oz. (30g)

With both these mixtures make up a solution with a dessertspoonful of the powder in a tumbler of water and leave the dentures to soak overnight.

TOOTHACHE REMEDY

Soak a swab of cotton wool with oil of cloves and hold against the area of pain. This will give temporary relief, but ultimately you will have to see your dentist!

SUNBURN LOTION

Although most of us are well aware of the power of the summer sun we nevertheless tend to overdo our first exposure in our impatience to get a tan, and the results are often quite painful. Here are two soothing lotions to try:

(i)
Zinc oxide	$\frac{1}{2}$ oz. (15g)
Borax	$\frac{1}{4}$ oz. (7g)
Glycerine	1 oz. (30g)
Lavender water	1 fl. oz. (30ml)
Distilled water	1 pt. (570ml)

Mix all together in a bottle or bottles and shake well before use. To apply, dab on the lotion and allow to dry.

(ii)
Colloidal kaolin	2 oz. (55g)
Calamine	$\frac{1}{2}$ oz. (15g)
Tincture of benzoin	$\frac{1}{2}$ oz. (15g)
Glycerine	$1\frac{1}{2}$ oz. (45g)
Gum tragacanth	$\frac{1}{8}$ oz. ($3\frac{1}{2}$g)
Distilled water	$1\frac{1}{4}$ pt. (710g)

Mix the kaolin, calamine and tragacanth, then add the tincture of benzoin, followed by the glycerine. Mix to a smooth consistency, slowly stir in the distilled water and bottle the lotion ready for use.

Note: The use of sun tan oil to protect pale bodies from the searing summer sun can obviate the need for the above – *see page 72.*

SMELLING SALTS

These classic revivers for bringing someone round from a faint can be prepared from:

(i)   Potassium carbonate grains $4\frac{1}{2}$ oz. (130g)
                   Ammonium carbonate grains   1 oz. (30g)
                   Ammonium chloride   4 oz. (115g)
                   Powdered camphor $\frac{1}{2}$ oz. (15g)
                   Oil of cloves   1 drop

Mix the ingredients together and keep in small bottles ready for emergencies.

(ii)   Ammonium carbonate pieces
                   Oil of lavender
                   Alcoholic solution of ammonia

Add a few drops of oil of lavender to about 2 fl. oz. (55ml) of the ammonia solution. Now fill a small bottle with ammonium carbonate pieces and moisten with the lavender oil/ammonia solution.

LINIMENT

Here is a simple embrocation which can be mixed at home. It is good for easing sprains.

                   Vinegar   1 cupful
                   Turpentine   1 cupful
                   Spirits of camphor   5 drops
                   Egg

Mix the vinegar, turpentine and camphor, break the egg and whisk all to a white and creamy consistency and keep in a bottle.

COSMETICS

BATH SALTS

Although bath salts tend to be a little out of fashion, they are nonetheless quite pleasant and can be both invigorating and relaxing.

A simple mixture, which can be made up from items in your larder, consists of:

Tartaric acid	10 oz. (285g)
Baking soda	9 oz. (255g)
Rice flour	6 oz. (170g)

Mix well together and take special care to keep in an air-tight jar. Sufficient can be added to the water at bath-time to suit your preference. It is an effervescent 'salt' and the carbon dioxide bubbles are refreshing to the skin.

BRAN BATH BAGS

Bran has always been popular with women famed for their fine satiny complexions. It's really soothing, especially to sunburned skin; it cleanses deeply and it makes the bath water soft and creamy.

Bran	4 oz. (115g)
Borax (powdered)	2 oz. (55g)
Castile or baby soap (grated)	1 oz. (30g)
or Soap flakes	1 oz. (30g)
Orris root (powdered)	1 oz. (30g)

Mix the above thoroughly together and add a few drops of your favourite bath oil. Now make some bags, about six inches square, from some porous white fabric, such as muslin or cheesecloth. Hem three sides of each bag and spoon in the mixture to the thickness of about half an inch. Sew up the bags, place one in the bath each day, and use it for washing as you would a sponge.

Alternatively, simply spoon some of the mixture into a square of muslin and tie it at the top in the style of a lavender bag, and use one of these each bath time.

HAND LOTION

(i) A good money saver which does the job as well as the bought products can be mixed from 1 oz. (30g) of glycerine and 3 fl. oz. (85ml) rose water, but it will not keep without a preservative and must be used as made. The consistency of the mixture is very slightly sticky and if the preference is for something less sticky the formula below can be tried:

(ii)	Gum tragacanth	$\frac{1}{4}$ oz. (7g)
	Glycerine	1 oz. (30g)
	Titanium dioxide	a pinch
	Water	8 oz. (225g)

First, allow the gum tragacanth to soak in the glycerine and water overnight (this is necessary as the gum tragacanth absorbs water very slowly) and then heat to 70°C. Now stir in the pinch of titanium dioxide and add a drop or two of your favourite perfume.

(iii) A hand softening 'ointment' can also be made from:

Lanolin	$\frac{5}{8}$ oz. ($17\frac{1}{2}$g)
Soft white paraffin	$1\frac{3}{4}$ oz. (50g)
Glycerine	$2\frac{1}{2}$ oz. (70g)

Melt the lanolin and paraffin together in a 'water bath' (*see page 11*) and then stir in the glycerine.

LOTION FOR CHAPPED HANDS

As a soothing lotion for hands that have succumbed to the ravages of winter's cold winds try the following:

Glycerine	1 fl. oz. (30ml)
Soap liniment	1 fl. oz. (30ml)
Distilled water to make	6 fl. oz. (170ml)

Shake the glycerine and soap liniment together well, add sufficient distilled water to make up to the required volume and shake well again.

FOOT DEODORANTS AND POWDERS

To make an effective foot deodorant take:

Aluminium chloride	1 oz. (30g)
Distilled water	$\frac{1}{4}$ pt. (140ml)

Dissolve the aluminium chloride in the distilled water and 'paint' or wipe on the solution each day after washing and thoroughly drying the feet.

There are a number of anti-fungal foot powders that can be made up quite simply. A good universal one is:

Alum	3 oz. (85g)
Talc (sterilized)	13 oz. (370g)

Ensure that the talc is sterilized and mix thoroughly with the powdered alum. The powder is now ready to dust on.

Other formulas include:

(i)	Salicylic acid powder	$\frac{1}{8}$ oz. ($3\frac{1}{2}$g)
	Talc (sterilized)	8 oz. (225g)
(ii)	Salicylic acid powder	$\frac{1}{4}$ oz. (7g)
	Boric acid	1 oz. (30g)
	Talc (sterilized)	8 oz. (225g)
(iii)	Salicylic acid powder	$\frac{1}{4}$ oz. (7g)
	Powdered zinc oleate	6 oz. (170g)
	Starch powder	12 oz. (340g)

A method of reviving aching feet is to immerse them in a weak solution of potassium permanganate (permanganate of potash) made up from a teaspoonful to every pint of water. The only snag is that it stains the feet, but if you don't mind this it is a useful and inexpensive anti-fungal and foot reviver.

HAIR SHAMPOO

Shampoos are not easy to make up in the home, and the ingredients are often difficult to obtain in small quantities. Nevertheless here are some mixtures to try:

(i)	Triethanolamine lauryl sulphate	1 fl. oz. (30ml)
	Distilled water	4 fl. oz. (115ml)

Triethanolamine lauryl sulphate foams readily in solution so carefully mix in with the water and add a drop or two of your favourite perfume. Triethanolamine lauryl sulphate is supplied in various concentrations and for shampoo purposes a 40% dilution is recommended.

(ii)	Sulphated castor oil	5 fl. oz. (140ml)
	Distilled water	5 fl. oz. (140ml)

Thoroughly mix the castor oil and water and add a trace of oil of pine.

HAIR SETTING LOTION

To make a setting lotion dissolve the following in a pint (570ml) of water.

Potassium carbonate	$\frac{1}{8}$ oz. ($3\frac{1}{2}$g)
Borax	$\frac{1}{8}$ oz. ($3\frac{1}{2}$g)
Ammonium carbonate	$\frac{1}{8}$ oz. ($3\frac{1}{2}$g)

Add a drop of perfume to suit, and the lotion is ready for use.

HAIR CONDITIONER

To give the hair a polished appearance, and to make it easy to comb, a conditioner such as this can be used:

Emulsifying wax	8 oz. (225g)
Hydrous lanolin	1 oz. (30g)
Citric acid	$\frac{1}{2}$ oz. (15g)
Water	1 pt. (570ml)

Dissolve the citric acid in the water and heat to 60°C–70°C. Separately, melt the wax and the lanolin together in a 'water bath' (*see page 11*) and add slowly to the citric acid solution. Allow to cool, stirring vigorously until set, and store in a jar. Apply to wet hair after shampooing.

SKIN AND HAIR LOTION

This can be used as a hair rinse or as a skin lotion.

Fresh rosemary	1 oz. (30g)
or dried rosemary	$\frac{1}{2}$ oz. (15g)
Distilled water	$\frac{1}{2}$ pt. (285ml)
Cider vinegar	$\frac{1}{2}$ pt. (285ml)

Put the rosemary and water in a saucepan and, having brought slowly to the boil, simmer gently for ten minutes. Now strain the liquid, mix with the cider vinegar and, when cool, pour into well stoppered bottles and keep in a cool, dark cupboard ready for use.

NAIL VARNISH

For those who like to experiment here is a formula to try, but take care as the ingredients are highly inflammable.

Dry pyroxylin	a pinch
Gum sandarac	a pinch
Acetone	1 oz. (30g)
Eosin	

Mix the pyroxylin, gum sandarac and acetone together and tint the varnish with a little eosin. The varnish should be kept in an air-tight bottle and can be applied in the usual way.

NAIL VARNISH REMOVER

Wherever there is nail varnish there has to be varnish remover, and a simple solvent can be mixed from these ingredients:

Amyl acetate	1 oz. (30g)
Acetone	1 oz. (30g)

Mix well, apply to the nails with a brush and wipe off before it dries.

NAIL STRENGTHENER

To strengthen brittle finger-nails try the following treatment:

Surgical spirit	$\frac{1}{2}$ pt. (285ml)
Castor oil	1 dessertspoonful

Put into a bottle and shake well before use. The idea is to dip your finger-nails into the solution after every wash.

CIGARETTE STAIN REMOVER

To remove those unsightly brown stains from a cigarette
smoker's fingers

Hydrogen peroxide (20 volumes)	$3\frac{1}{4}$ oz. (90g)
Distilled water	$1\frac{3}{4}$ oz. (50g)
Alcoholic solution of ammonia	$\frac{1}{2}$ oz. (15g)

Mix the ingredients together in a bottle and shake well before
use. Store in a dark glass bottle, and keep in a cool place out of
direct sunshine.

MILKY 'DRINK' FOR THIRSTY SKINS

In days gone by, buttermilk was the beauty secret of queens
and commoners alike; including any dairy-maid whose face
was her fortune. Take a tip from those 'lovelies' of long ago,
using dried milk powder (which is equivalent to the milk left
over after making butter).

Dried milk powder	1 tablespoonful
Sunflower oil	
or Almond oil	1 teaspoonful

Mix the two ingredients together, adding water drop by drop
until a creamy paste is formed. Apply to the face, leave until the
mixture dries, then rinse off.

This simple treatment refines the skin, making it smooth,
clear and supple; giving that 'brilliant complexion' so much
admired through the ages.

If your skin is greasy, omit the oil, and use only a
tablespoonful of milk powder and a teaspoonful of water to
make up the mixture. You may have to add a few drops more
water to get the right consistency.

TOOTHPASTE

Although some of the ingredients might be difficult to find, here is a toothpaste to try:

Chalk	4 oz. (115g)
Sodium lauryl sulphate	1 teaspoonful
Glycerine	2 oz. (55g)
Sodium carragheenate	1 teaspoonful
Saccharin	1 teaspoonful
Water	4 fl. oz. (115ml)

First mix the glycerine and about 1 fl. oz. (30ml) of the water together, then add the saccharin and sodium carragheenate, stirring well. Slowly mix in the sodium lauryl sulphate and chalk. At this point a flavouring of your choice can be added — say one or two drops of oil of peppermint or oil of cloves. Finally, add the rest of the water, mixing thoroughly.

TOOTHPOWDER

Tooth powders are easier and cheaper to produce. Their essential properties are cleaning power without abrasive action, some antiseptic quality, and a lack of any unpleasant taste or smell.

Precipitated chalk	$4\frac{1}{2}$ oz. (130g)
Dental soap	$\frac{1}{4}$ oz. (7g)
Saccharin	a pinch

Mix all three together thoroughly and, if preferred, add one or two drops of oil of peppermint or oil of cloves to flavour.

TOOTH WHITENER

To remove obstinate stains and to whiten the teeth rub with a linen handkerchief slightly moistened with '10 volume' hydrogen peroxide.

RICHER COLD CREAM

This one is more expensive to produce, as one might expect, but it is a pure cream made out of oils and waxes without the use of water, so there is less risk of it 'going off' with keeping.

White beeswax	½ oz. (15g)
Spermaceti	1 oz. (30g)
Almond oil	4 fl. oz. (115ml)
Borax	⅛ oz. (3½g)
Perfume	as required

Using a 'water bath' dissolve the borax in the almond oil over a low heat, and then dissolve the wax and spermaceti in this mixture. Add perfume as required, and stir vigorously until cool.

COLD CREAM

Here is a good standard mixture for cold cream. It consists of an oil in water emulsion, but in the absence of a long-term preservative it is advisable to make small quantities only and to keep in the fridge when not in use.

White beeswax	1 oz. (30g)
Borax	⅛ oz. (3½g)
Light liquid paraffin B.P.	4 fl. oz. (115ml)
Distilled water	1½ fl. oz. (45ml)
Perfume	as required

Use a 'water bath' (*see page 11*) for this one. Put the liquid paraffin in the basin and stand the 'water bath' over a low heat. When warm, dissolve the beeswax in the paraffin, stirring all the time. Now dissolve the borax in the distilled water at the same temperature as the wax/paraffin mixture, and gradually stir this in to the mixture. Remove from heat and stir vigorously until cold. Perfume can be added as required.

Note: Care in equalizing the temperatures before mixing together the borax solution and the wax/paraffin mixture will ensure a smooth cream.

SKIN TONIC

A simple skin tonic can be made up from:

Rose water	¼ pt. (140ml)
Witch hazel	¼ pt. (140ml)

Mix well together and bottle ready for use.

SUN TAN OIL

You can make up your own sun tan oil from the following:

Egg yolk	
Olive oil	1 cupful
Cider vinegar	1 tablespoonful
Wheat germ oil	1 tablespoonful

Blend all well together and apply in the usual way.

ASTRINGENT LOTION

Here is an astringent lotion that can be made up and used as an 'after shave'. The formula does not include any long-term preservative, so don't make gallons and expect it to keep for months. It will last for a short while, though, as the borax in the mixture gives it some protection.

Powdered alum	¼ oz. (7g)
Boric acid powder	⅛ oz. (3½g)
Tincture of benzoin	½ teaspoonful (2ml)
Glycerine	1½ teaspoonsful (7½ml)
Rosewater	2½ fl. oz. (75ml)
Distilled water to make	5 fl. oz. (150ml)

Dissolve the alum and boric acid powder in about 2 fl. oz. (60ml) distilled water. Add the glycerine and rosewater, and finally the tincture of benzoin. Shake well and add sufficient distilled water to make up to 5 fl. oz. (150ml). Leave to stand for a few hours before straining through fine gauze or calico into a bottle ready for use.

HANDICRAFTS

GLUES

(i) A good strong all-purpose glue for paper and card, which can also be used for jointing wood can be made up from the following. It is quite quick drying and is particularly useful for modelling with card, or for making paper decorations.

Gum arabic (powder)	$1\frac{1}{4}$ oz. (35g)
Starch (soluble)	1 oz. (30g)
Sugar	2 teaspoonsful
Camphor	1 teaspoonful

To mix this up you will need a 'water bath' (*see page 11*). While the 'water bath' heats up dissolve the gum arabic in about $1\frac{1}{2}$ oz. of water, adding the powder gradually and stirring in to prevent too much clogging. Now separately dissolve the starch in a similar quantity of water and when in solution add to the gum arabic and stir in the sugar and camphor. Pour the mixture into the basin in the 'water bath' and keep the water simmering, stirring the glue until it forms an even consistency. Decant into a warm jar and allow to cool.

(ii) Another glue which is extremely strong and dries very quickly on application: good for paper and wood.

Borax	$\frac{1}{2}$ oz. (15g)
Dextrine (pale yellow)	5 oz. (140g)
Glucose	$\frac{1}{2}$ oz. (15g)

Dissolve the borax in about $4\frac{1}{2}$ fl. oz. (130ml) of hot water, add the dextrine and glucose and heat gently, stirring all the time, until all ingredients are dissolved. At no time should the temperature of the solution exceed 90°C. A check can be kept on this by using a cooking thermometer or something similar (*see page 12*). There will be some loss of water during heating, and this should be replaced. When fully mixed filter the solution through a cloth (a flannel will do) into a suitable container.

(iii) This one is for use in woodwork and is based on the raw glue that can be bought dry from a hardware store:

Sugar	2 oz. (55g)
Slaked lime	$\frac{1}{2}$ oz. (15g)
Glue	2 oz. (55g)

Dissolve the sugar in a cupful of warm water, add the lime stirring continuously. Leave this to settle for a few days and then decant the clear solution and soak the dry glue in this for about 24 hours. Now heat the mixture in a 'water bath' (*see page 11*) until fully dissolved.

(iv) Another wood glue:

Calcium chloride	$\frac{1}{2}$ oz. (15g)
Glue	$2\frac{1}{2}$ oz. (70g)

Soak the ingredients together in about 2 fl. oz. (55ml) of water for twelve hours, then heat in a 'water bath' (*see page 11*) until fully dissolved.

PERSPEX CEMENT

Scraps of perspex can be dissolved in chloroform to form a 'dope' like substance which acts as a cement for joining sheets of perspex. The mixture is non-inflammable, but chloroform is, of course, dangerous and should not be inhaled.

WOOD STAINS

Here are some do-it-yourself wood stains for the handyman. In all cases it is advisable to wear rubber gloves during application to avoid staining your hands.

(i) **Ebony**

Sodium dichromate	$3\frac{1}{2}$ oz. (100g)
Gallic acid	$\frac{1}{2}$ oz. (15g)

Dissolve the sodium dichromate in about $1\frac{3}{4}$ pt. (995ml) of hot water and apply the solution sparingly to the surface to be stained. Now dissolve the gallic acid in about $1\frac{3}{4}$ pt. (995ml) hot water, and when the first coat has dried apply this solution. Keep repeating this process, alternating the solutions, until the desired degree of blackness is obtained.

A dull finish can be imparted by rubbing the finished job with a rag moistened with a trace of linseed oil. Alternatively, a gloss finish can be achieved by varnishing.

(ii) **Nutwood**

Dissolve 1 oz. (30g) of potassium permanganate in 2 pt. (1135ml) of water and apply two coats to the surface to be stained. Leave for five minutes after which wash over with water and allow to dry.

(iii) Oak

Dissolve sufficient potassium dichromate in cold water to achieve the depth of colouring required, and apply several coats of the solution to the surface for staining.

(iv) Walnut

Potassium permanganate	3 oz. (85g)
Magnesium sulphate (Epsom salts)	3 oz. (85g)

Dissolve the above in 2 pt. (1135ml) hot water and apply two coats of the solution to the wood. The potassium permanganate decomposes while in contact with the wood to result in the walnut colouring.

AN EFFECTIVE VARNISH REMOVER

To clean the varnish off old furniture make up a mixture of equal quantities of turpentine and methylated spirit. Keep in a well-stoppered bottle and shake hard before use. The mixture has a solvent effect and is best applied with a rag wrapped round a swab of cotton wool.

FRENCH POLISH

The most important ingredients when french polishing are skill and patience. The rest can include:

Shellac	8 oz. (225g)
Benzoin	$\frac{1}{4}$ oz. (7g)
Sandarac	$\frac{1}{2}$ oz. (15g)
Industrial methylated spirit	2 pt. (1135ml)

Pour the methylated spirit into a bottle or bottles, chop up the shellac, benzoin and sandarac, add to the methylated spirit and leave to dissolve. When in solution, give the bottle a good shake and the polish will be ready for use.

Before applying the polish, rub over the wood with a little linseed oil, removing any excess with a soft cloth. Saturate a piece of cotton wool with the french polish, cover with a piece of linen, and rub the wool gently with a circular motion. If the varnish becomes sticky during application of the polish, add a drop of linseed oil to the pad before continuing.

To provide a mirror finish, after the polish has been applied rub over with a linen cloth moistened with a little absolute alcohol. Rub briskly as the alcohol evaporates.

ALLOYS

For the ambitious man with a forge in his garage here are some
suggestions for metallic alloys for model making etc.

Art bronzes

(i)	Copper	$8\frac{1}{2}$ parts
	Zinc	1 part
	Tin	$\frac{1}{2}$ part
(ii)	Copper	$8\frac{1}{2}$ parts
	Zinc	1 part
	Tin	$\frac{1}{4}$ part
	Lead	$\frac{1}{4}$ part
(iii)	Copper	8 parts
	Zinc	$1\frac{1}{2}$ parts
	Tin	$\frac{1}{2}$ part

Medallion alloy

(i)	Tin	3 parts
	Lead	13 parts
	Bismuth	6 parts
(ii)	Tin	3 parts
	Lead	4 parts
	Bismuth	7 parts
(iii)	Copper	5 parts
	Zinc	4 parts
	Nickel	1 part

Pewter

(i)	Tin	8 parts
	Antimony	$1\frac{1}{2}$ parts
	Lead	$\frac{1}{2}$ part
(ii)	Tin	4 parts
	Lead	1 part

PAPIER MACHE

An extremely versatile modelling material is papier maché. Basically this is just soggy paper 'mashed' together so that it can be formed into the required shape and then allowed to harden on drying. The 'mash' can be strengthened and made more malleable by the addition of plaster of paris and glue as follows:

Dry paper	1 oz. (30g)
Water	3 fl. oz. (85ml)
Plaster of paris	8 oz. (225g)
Glue	$4\frac{1}{2}$ tablespoonsful

Quantities can be increased in proportion in accordance with requirements.

Firstly, tear up the paper into strips or small pieces and soak in the water. Meanwhile, melt the glue. When the paper has become thoroughly saturated squeeze gently to remove any excess water and put the pulp into a mixing bowl and add about 3 tablespoonsful of the melted glue, stirring the mass into a sticky paste. Now add about a third of the plaster of paris, mixing thoroughly until the paste is so dry and thick that it is difficult to work. At this point add the rest of the glue, still mixing, and then the remainder of the plaster of paris. Thoroughly mix the mass with the fingers until it is finely kneaded and free from lumps. If the mix is too dry, add a few drops of water and knead again.

When moulded, the papier maché will dry within 2 to 3 hours, but any unused material can be kept moist by wrapping it in a wet cloth.

CANDLE-MAKING

This is a fascinating hobby, and there is unlimited scope for experimentation and inventiveness. The basic requirements are wax, stearine and suitable colourings, while the shapes are dependent upon the moulds you use. You will, of course, also need suitable material for wicks, and all these things can be found in the better handicraft shop. However, if improvisation is your strong point, you may be able to devise your own equipment and colouring.

Here is a 'recipe' to try:

> Hydroxystearic acid
> Stearine
> Paraffin wax

You will need a 'water bath' (*see page 11*) to melt the wax in. When melted, stir in a 3 to 1 mixture of the hydroxystearic acid and stearine to the desired consistency. Add colouring of your choice, stir in, and pour molten wax into the mould (the wick being suspended in the middle of the mould). When set, break out of the mould and trim off any waste ready for use.

HOME-MADE SCRAP PADS

Note-books can be expensive to buy, especially when all you may want them for is to jot down your shopping list or record 'phone messages. You can make your own 'jotters' quite easily with the help of the glue recipe at the beginning of this section.

All you need is some loose scrap paper. If you don't have any about the house, ask around. Your local printer may have some 'off-cuts' which he may be only too pleased to get rid of. Knock the paper down and, taking a pile about half an inch thick, apply a liberal coating of glue to one edge. Now wrap a piece of paper round the glued edge and leave to dry under a heavy weight. Once set the glue will hold the sheets of the pad together like a book.

MODELLING WAX

Wax is also an ideal medium for modelling, and some interesting set pieces can be made up, such as artificial flower arrangements and the traditional bowls of wax fruit.

The main requirement is that the wax be malleable at 'hand temperature' and that when worked it will hold its shape.

White beeswax	2 oz. (55g)
Turpentine	$\frac{1}{2}$ fl. oz. (15ml)
Sesame oil	1 teaspoonful

Break up the beeswax into small pieces and work in the turpentine and sesame oil until a plastic mass is obtained. To assist the kneading process the wax can be warmed by placing it in warm water. Colouring dyes will have to be added during the mixing process according to requirements.

'FIXING' DRAWINGS

Pencil sketches are very prone to smudging, and to prevent this they should be 'fixed' with a very light coat of sealer or varnish.

This can be done by lightly brushing with isinglass solution, or by using this more elaborate formula:

Shellac	2 teaspoonsful
Sandarac	1 teaspoonful
Industrial methylated spirit	$4\frac{1}{4}$ fl. oz. (130ml)

TO SHARPEN SCISSORS

A simple trick is to cut through pieces of fine sandpaper. The abrasiveness of the paper acts as a sort of grindstone and makes dull blades sharp again.

AQUARIUM MAKING/REPAIRS

The main problem when making an aquarium is in making it water tight, and the answer to it lies in the putty-like adhesive used to seal the glass panels to the framework. Both the fish within and the housewife without have a vested interest in the effectiveness of your handiwork in this direction, so it would be well worthwhile to have a few 'dummy runs' before committing your pet piranha to the finished job!

Here are some mixtures to try:

| (i) | Glycerine | 4 oz. (115g) |
| | Litharge | 4 oz. (115g) |

Mix thoroughly to a paste. Use within ten minutes. The paste will set hard in about three hours.

(ii)	Powdered glass	4 oz. (115g)
	Litharge	2 oz. (55g)
	Boiled linseed oil	2 fl. oz. (55ml)

Heat the linseed oil and stir in the litharge and powdered glass. Apply while still hot.

(iii)	Litharge	2 oz. (55g)
	Plaster of paris	2 oz. (55g)
	Manganese borate	1 teaspoonful
	Fine white sand	2 oz. (55g)
	Colophony (powdered)	7 oz. (200g)
	Boiled linseed oil	

Mix together the powders thoroughly. Stir in linseed oil until the mixture forms a stiff paste.

(iv)	Flowers of sulphur	1 oz. (30g)
	Ammonium chloride	1 oz. (30g)
	Iron filings	1 oz. (30g)
	Boiled linseed oil	
	White lead	

Mix the flowers of sulphur, ammonium chloride and iron filings together, and add boiled linseed oil to make a runny mixture. Mix in sufficient white lead to make a thin paste.

INVISIBLE INK

Although superseded in the world of international espionage by the microdot and other sophisticated developments born of the technological age, invisible ink still has a certain charm as a means of indulging in covert correspondence. There are a number of recipes for making such ink, but here is one to try:

Cobalt chloride	2 oz. (55g)
Glycerine	$\frac{1}{2}$ fl. oz. (15ml)
Water to make	1 pt. (570ml)

Use a dip-pen for writing the 'secret' letter. Upon receipt the addressee can make visible the text by gently heating the apparently blank sheet of paper.

CLEANING OIL PAINTINGS

First a word of warning. Oil paintings can easily be damaged in untrained hands, and so the treatment of valuable works of art should always be left to experts. Less important paintings can be treated at home – often with a surprising degree of success.

To begin with, give the picture a wash with soap and water, and rinse off with clean water. This operation will remove the surface dirt, but it may be necessary to repeat the process a number of times if the picture is particularly dirty. Now wipe the surface of the painting very gently with a wad of cotton wool dipped in pure linseed oil to brighten up the colours.

POT-POURRI

A pot-pourri is easily made, and if you are good at pottery there is unlimited scope for creating decorative and shapely containers for the dried-petal mixtures. A jar will do just as well, though; or any other suitable container.

First of all, collect a variety of petals from your favourite sweet-smelling flowers, then lay them out to dry in a warm place out of direct sunlight. Try lilac, rose and lavender. After they have dried mix with equal parts of orris root powder and put into an air-tight jar. Leave in a dark place for two weeks or so, after which the contents can be put in containers ready for service about the house.

IN THE GARAGE

ANTI-FREEZE

An expensive, but nevertheless necessary, item needed each winter by the car owner is anti-freeze. Generally, commercial solutions are based on glycol, but you can make up your own with glycerine and water.

To protect down to about −5°C mix 1 pt. (570ml) glycerine to every 4 pt (2280ml) water. For greater protection the proportion of glycerine should be increased. A mixture of 2 parts glycerine to 3 parts water protects down to −15°C, and 2 parts glycerine to 1 part water does not freeze until −46°C. It is not advisable to increase the glycerine content beyond this as frost protection tends to lessen rather than improve.

An alternative mixture is 2 parts glycerine, 3 parts potassium carbonate and 4 parts water. This solution should protect down to -30°C.

Finally a mixture which is closer to the commercial anti-freeze. Use 1 part ethylene glycol to 4 parts water (as a rust inhibitor 1% sodium nitrate can be added). This gives protection down to −8°C and for greater protection the proportion of glycol should be increased.

CAR POLISH

Making your own car polish will probably not save you any money, unless you intend making large quantities, but if you have ready access to the ingredients and if you are enthusiastic enough there will be a certain satisfaction from being self-sufficient. Here are two 'recipes' to try:

(i)		
Naphtha	$6\frac{1}{2}$ oz. (185g)
Bentonite	$1\frac{1}{2}$ oz. (45g)
Triethanolamine	$\frac{1}{4}$ oz. (7g)
Beeswax	1 oz. (30g)
Ceresine	1 oz. (30g)
Stearic acid	$\frac{3}{4}$ oz. (21g)
Water	$6\frac{1}{2}$ fl. oz. (185ml)

Mix together the stearic acid, triethanolamine and water and heat to boiling, stirring to a smooth solution. Separately melt the beeswax and ceresine in the naphtha (using a 'water bath' — *see page 11*), and add this mixture to the first solution. Now stir thoroughly until the mixture is smooth, add the bentonite, and continue stirring until a creamy paste is formed. The polish can now be tinned and kept ready for use.

(ii)	Carnauba wax	3 oz. (85g)
	Paraffin wax	1 oz. (30g)
	Glyceryl monostearate	1 oz. (30g)
	Solvent naphtha	1 oz. (30g)
	Turpentine	2 oz. (55g)
	Borax	1 oz. (30g)
	Water	$7\frac{1}{2}$ fl. oz. (210ml)

Melt the carnauba wax and paraffin wax together in a 'water bath' (*see page 11*), taking care not to allow the temperature to exceed 115°C. Add the glyceryl monostearate and, when melted, stir in the solvent naphtha and turpentine. Separately, dissolve the borax in boiling water and add slowly to the first mixture, whisking or stirring vigorously.

RUST INHIBITOR

The fight against rust is an endless one, and generally speaking it is a losing battle. However, there are various methods of protection which can be used, and the useful life of metal parts exposed to the weather can be adequately prolonged with a little care and attention. It is best to get in before rust starts to form, and coat the surface with a waterproof material. For example, a simple method is to dissolve some wax in turpentine (in the same way as the basic floor polish – *see page 20*) and apply to the metal parts to be protected. The idea is that as the turpentine evaporates it leaves a hard layer of wax on the surface of the metal, thereby sealing it off from the air.

RUST REMOVERS

If the rust has got there before you, as it so often has, here are some measures to adopt:

(i) Rust which has only recently formed may be removed by rubbing with a cork covered in oil, but this would only do for small and slightly affected areas.

(ii) For rust which has become more established try:

Tripoli	1 oz. (30g)
Flowers of sulphur	1 oz. (30g)
Olive oil	

Mix the tripoli and sulphur together, and add olive oil to the powder to form a paste. This can then be applied to the rust outbreak with a rag, and a little brisk rubbing should clean up the affected area. It would be particularly useful for cleaning chrome parts, but would not be able to tackle really advanced cases of rust encrustation.

(iii) Treat the rust with olive oil and leave for a few days to soak in. Then rub down with emery paper, wipe clean and finally rub with fine graphite on a piece of chamois leather.

(iv) Apply a hot, saturated solution of sodium pyrophosphate. Leave for a little while and then wash off with warm water.

(v)	Potassium acid tartrate	1 oz. (30g)
	Sodium acetate	1 oz. (30g)

Dissolve the potassium acid tartrate in a pint (570ml) of hot water, and brush this on to the rust. Wash off, apply a solution of the sodium acetate in a pint (570ml) of water, and wash again.

HAND CLEANER

Hands ingrained with oil and grease are difficult to clean with ordinary soap, but the following mixtures are effective:

(i)   Soft soap   3 oz. (85g)
       Oil of turpentine   1 pt. (570ml)

Melt down the soft soap in a 'water bath' (*see page 11*) and add the turpentine little by little stirring all the time. To use, rub into the hands and wash off with warm water. A little glycerine can be added as a smoothing agent.

(ii) A more abrasive mixture:

           Powdered soap $3\frac{1}{2}$ oz. (100g)
           Waterglass   1oz. (30g)
           Pumice powder $\frac{1}{2}$ oz. (15g)
           Kaolin   5 oz. (140g)

Mix the ingredients together thoroughly until a paste is formed. Rub on to the hands and wash off with warm water.

(iii)   Borax (powdered) $2\frac{1}{2}$ oz. (70g)
        Pumice (finely powdered)   1 teaspoonful
        Hard soap (finely powdered) $1\frac{1}{2}$ oz. (45g)

Mix the powders thoroughly. Rub on to the hands and wash off with warm water.

WATERPROOFING CANVAS

Here is a useful mixture for re-waterproofing leaky tents or sports car hoods, and it can be 'painted' on with a brush.

Gelatin (powder)	$\frac{3}{4}$ oz. (21g)
Alum	$\frac{1}{2}$ oz. (15g)

Mix the gelatin powder in half a pint (285ml) of water, and separately mix the alum in another half pint of water. Now heat the gelatin solution to about 40°C and apply to the canvas with a brush. Allow to dry, and apply a coat of the alum solution.

If the leak in the canvas is confined to a very small area, a quick and easy method is to rub the underside with a lump of beeswax until the surface develops a uniform white or grayish appearance.

WATERPROOFING WOOD

To render wood resistant to water it can be treated with the following:

Boric acid	$\frac{1}{2}$ oz. (15g)
Ammonium chloride	$\frac{1}{2}$ oz. (15g)
Sodium borate	$\frac{1}{4}$ oz. (7g)

Dissolve all three in half a pint (285ml) of water and soak the wood in the mixture.

Alternatively the wood to be treated can be soaked in a solution of zinc chloride.

SOLDER

There are many varieties of solder, each one with its particular use, but the type most commonly used in the home for soldering electrical connections, and perhaps for model making, is a soft solder with a relatively low melting point. Basically, such solder is an alloy of tin and lead, although bismuth is sometimes included. If you have the means to fuse together the component metals, here are some solders to make:

(i)   Tin   5 parts
         Lead   2 parts
The amalgam has a melting point of 180°C.

(ii)   Tin   1 part
         Lead   1 part
The amalgam has a melting point of 200°C.

(iii)   Bismuth   2 parts
         Tin   1 part
         Lead   1 part
The amalgam has a melting point of 200°C.

(iv)   Tin   1 part
         Lead   2 parts
The amalgam has a melting point of 240°C.

Flux

To ease the adherence and fusibility of solder a substance known as 'flux' is used, and such a substance can be made up from:

Zinc chloride	2¾ oz. (78g)
Ammonium chloride	1 oz. (30g)
Water	6¼ fl. oz. (175ml)

Dissolve the chlorides in the water, and paint on some of the solution to the job to be soldered.

IN THE GARDEN

WEEDKILLER

Here are two weedkillers which, although perhaps not as instantly effective as some, are relatively non-toxic to humans. Nevertheless, care should be taken to keep all mixtures in clearly marked bottles, and out of reach of small children.

| (i) | Copper sulphate | 1 oz. (30g) |
| | Water | $\frac{1}{2}$ pt. (285ml) |

Mix thoroughly. Add 1 pt. (570ml) of this mixture to each bucketful of water.

(ii)	Ferrous sulphate	1 oz. (30g)
	Alum	1 oz. (30g)
	Water	$1\frac{1}{2}$ pt. (850ml)

Mix thoroughly before application.

FERTILIZERS

Plants require a variety of inorganic mineral constituents which are normally supplied from the soil via the root system of the plant. Twelve of these essential mineral elements are generally recognized for the plant's well-being, i.e. nitrogen, phosphorus, sulphur, potassium, calcium, magnesium, iron, zinc, copper, manganese, boron and molybdenum. The first six of these can be said to be the *major elements*, and are included in some form in nearly all artificial fertilizers.

Indoor plants

(i)
Common salt	10 oz. (285g)
Potassium nitrate	5 oz. (140g)
Magnesium sulphate (Epsom salts)	5 oz. (140g)
Sodium phosphate	2 oz. (55g)
Magnesia	1 oz. (30g)

Mix thoroughly and bottle. Dissolve a teaspoonful in 2 pt. (1135ml) water.

(ii)
Ammonium nitrate	4 oz. (115g)
Potassium nitrate	9 oz. (255g)
Ammonium phosphate	5 oz. (140g)

Mix thoroughly. About 2g dissolved in water is sufficient for a medium-sized plant pot.

(iii)
Sodium phosphate	1¼ lb. (570g)
Ammonium sulphate	10 oz. (285g)
Common salt	10 oz. (285g)
Potassium nitrate	5 oz. (140g)
Magnesium sulphate (Epsom Salts)	5 oz. (140g)
Magnesium carbonate	1 oz. (30g)

Mix thoroughly. Add one teaspoonful to 2 pt. (1135ml) water.

(iv)   Ammonium nitrate   1 lb. (455g)
Ammonium phosphate   8 oz. (225g)
Calcium sulphate   2 oz. (55g)
Ammonium chloride   2 oz. (55g)
Ferrous sulphate   2 oz. (55g)

Mix thoroughly and dissolve 2 parts in 1000 parts of water.

(v)   Ammonium nitrate   7 oz. (200g)
Potassium phosphate   5 oz. (140g)
Potassium nitrate   4 oz. (115g)
Ammonium sulphate   2 oz. (55g)

Mix well. This mixture is particularly good for the leaves of the plant; for flowering plants omit the ammonium nitrate.

Outdoor plants

(i)   Ammonium sulphate   1 lb. (455g)
Potassium nitrate $\frac{1}{2}$ lb. (225g)
Sugar $\frac{1}{4}$ lb. (115g)

Mix thoroughly. Dissolve one teaspoonful in each gallon of water used.

(ii)   Sodium phosphate   4 oz. (115g)
Common salt   2 oz. (55g)
Potassium nitrate   1 oz. (30g)
Magnesium sulphate (Epsom salts)   1 oz. (30g)

Mix thoroughly. Dissolve one teaspoonful in 2 pt. (1135ml) water.

(iii)   Calcium superphosphate $4\frac{1}{2}$ oz. (130g)
Fine bone meal $3\frac{1}{2}$ oz. (100g)
Ammonium sulphate $1\frac{3}{4}$ oz. (50g)
Potassium sulphate $1\frac{1}{2}$ oz. (45g)

Mix thoroughly and add direct to the soil.

104

(iv) For roses

Calcium superphosphate	$5\frac{3}{4}$ oz. (160g)
Fine bone meal	$9\frac{1}{2}$ oz. (270g)
Potassium sulphate	4 oz. (115g)
Ammonium sulphate	3 oz. (85g)
Ferric oxide	$\frac{1}{2}$ oz. (15g)

Mix thoroughly and add direct to the soil.

(v) For tomatoes

| Ammonium sulphate | 9 oz. (255g) |
| Ferrous sulphate | 1 oz. (30g) |

This mixture is suitable as a general fertilizer for tomatoes. At the time of transplanting, a mixture of equal parts of calcium superphosphate and bone meal should be used. When the flowers are set, a top dressing of 6 parts calcium superphosphate to 1 part ammonium sulphate should be used.

INSECTICIDES

To contain the destruction to plants caused each year by pests here is some ammunition to add to your armoury. A good spray is needed for successful application.

(i)	Paraffin oil	2 pt. (1135ml)
	Soap	1 oz. (30g)
	Water	1 pt. (570ml)

Dissolve the soap in the water and boil. Add immediately to the paraffin oil and whisk until a perfect emulsion is formed.

Dilute 1 part of the mixture to 15 parts water for ordinary insects. For scale insects, the mixture should be diluted with 9 parts water, and for soft insects such as plant lice, the mixture should be diluted with 20–25 parts water. Use a spray to apply.

(ii)	Green soap	3 oz. (85g)
	Linseed oil	2 oz. (55g)
	Carbolic acid	1 oz. (30g)

Thoroughly mix the soap, linseed oil and carbolic acid. Then stir into about 4 gallons of water and spray on to plants.

| (iii) | Carbolic acid | 1 oz. (30g) |
| | Water glass | 1¼ pt. (710ml) |

Thoroughly mix and spray on to plants.

(iv) Beetle powder

	Cocoa powder	1 oz. (30g)
	Starch	2 oz. (55g)
	Borax	9 oz. (255g)

Mix thoroughly and dust on to plants.

RAT POISON

The use of poisons containing potassium cyanide, strychnine, phosphorus and arsenic are outside the scope of this book, but nevertheless there are several other formulations which can be mixed in comparative safety. All the mixtures here should of course be kept well away from children and pets.

Some of the formulas contain squill. This is not particularly dangerous to humans and domestic animals, but is classified as a poison and it may therefore be necessary to sign the chemist's poison register on purchasing it. While the poison is taking effect the rat will seek water, and so it is advisable not to allow access to water which is for household use.

Note that powdered squill rapidly picks up moisture, and so should be stored in a closed container when not required for use.

(i)	Red squill powder	1 oz. (30g)
	Fine oatmeal	$2\frac{1}{2}$ oz. (70g)
	Dripping	$1\frac{1}{2}$ oz. (45g)

Melt the dripping and mix it thoroughly with the squill powder and oatmeal to form a thick paste. Leave in a suitable place.

(ii)	Red squill powder	2 oz. (55g)
	Bread	3 oz. (85g)
	Dripping	3 oz. (85g)
	Syrup	2 oz. (55g)
	Oil of anise	5-6 drops

Crumble the bread and mix the ingredients to a paste. A sufficient quantity to use is a volume about the size of a marble.

(iii)   Red squill powder   1 oz. (30g)
         Barium carbonate   4 oz. (115g)
         Oil of anise   5 drops
Mix thoroughly.

(iv)   Barium carbonate powder   1 oz. (30g)
         Cheese, grated   1 oz. (30g)
         Dripping   1 oz. (30g)
         Fine oatmeal   1 oz. (30g)
Melt the dripping and mix it thoroughly with the other
ingredients to form a thick paste. The dose is 1 teaspoonful for
rats, and $\frac{1}{2}$ teaspoonful for mice.

SOURCES OF SUPPLY

C=Chemist; H=Hardware Store; G=Grocer

Acetone, C
Alcoholic solution of ammonia, C
Almond oil, C
Alum, C
Aluminium chloride, C
Ammonia, H or C
Ammonium borate, C
Ammonium carbonate, C
Ammonium chloride (Sal ammoniac), C
Ammonium nitrate, C
Ammonium phosphate, C
Ammonium sulphate, C
Ammonia alum, C
Amyl acetate, C
Antimony, Metal merchant

Baking soda (sodium bicarbonate), G
Barium carbonate, C
Beeswax, H or C
Bentonite, C
Benzene, C
Benzoin, C
Bismuth, Metal merchant
Bone meal, H or Garden shop
Borax, C
Boric acid, C
Bran, G

Calamine, C
Calcium chloride, C
Calcium sulphate, C
Camphor, C
Caraway seeds, G
Carbolic acid, C
Carbon tetrachloride, H or C
Carnauba wax, C
Castor oil, G or C
Caustic soda, H or C
Ceresine, C
Chalk, H
Charcoal, H or C
China clay, C
Chlorate of lime, C
Chlorinated lime, C
Chloroform, C
Cider vinegar, G or C
Cinnamon, G
Citric acid, C
Cloves, G
Cobalt chloride, C
Colloidal kaolin, C
Colophony, C
Copper, Metal merchant

Dental soap, C
Dextrine, C
Dimethyl phthalate, C

Emulsifying wax, C
Eosin, C
Epsom salts, C
Ethylene glycol, C
Eucalyptus oil, C

Ferric oxide, C
Ferrous sulphate, C
Flowers of sulphur, C
Fuller's earth, C

Gallic acid, C
Gelatin powder, G or C
Glue, H
Glucose, C
Glycerine, C
Glyceryl monostearate, C
Graphite, H or C
Gum arabic, C
Gum tragacanth, C

Honey, G
Hydrogen peroxide, C
Hydrostearic acid, C
Hydrous lanolin, C

Industrial methylated spirit, H
Iron filings, H
Iron oxide, C

Kaolin, C

Lanolin, C
Lavender water, C
Lead, Metal Merchant
Levigated chalk, C
Linseed oil, H
Litharge, H or C

Mace, G
Manganese borate, C
Manganese chloride, C
Magnesia, C
Magnesium carbonate, C
Magnesium sulphate (Epsom salts), C
Methylated spirit, H

Naphtha, C
Nickel, Metal merchant
Nutmeg, G

Oil of anise, C
Oil of camphor, C
Oil of cassia, C
Oil of cloves, C
Oil of peppermint, C
Oleic acid, C
Olive oil, G
Orris root, G
Orthophosphoric acid, C
Oxalic acid, C

Paraffin, H
Paraffin, soft white, C
Paraffin oil, C
Paraffin wax, C
Peppermint water, C
Plaster of paris, C
Potassium acid tartrate, C
Potassium carbonate, C
Potassium nitrate (saltpetre), C
Potassium permanganate, C
Precipitated chalk, C
Pumice powder, H or C
Pyroxylin, C

Red lead, H
Rice flour, G
Rosemary, G
Rose water, C
Rosin powder, H or C
Rye flour, G

Saccharin, C
Saliscylic acid powder, C
Sandarac, H or C
Saponine, C
Shellac, H or C
Slaked lime, H or C
Sodium acetate, C
Sodium borate, C
Sodium carragheenate, C
Sodium dichromate, C
Sodium lauryl sulphate, C
Sodium nitrate, C
Sodium perborate, C
Sodium percarbonate, C
Sodium phosphate, C
Sodium pyrophosphate, C
Sodium silicate, C
Sodium thiosulphate (hypo), C or
    Photographic shop
Spermaceti, C
Spirits of camphor, C
Squill, C
Starch, G
Stearic acid, C
Stearine, C or Handicraft shop
Sulphated castor oil, C
Surgical spirit, C

Talc (sterilized), C
Tartaric acid (Cream of Tartar),
    G or C

Tin, Metal merchant
Tincture of benzoin, C
Turpentine, H
Titanium dioxide, C
Triethanolamine, C
Triethanolamine lauryl sulphate, C
Tripoli, C
Trisodium phosphate, C

Washing soda, G
Waterglass, C
Wheat germ oil, G or Health Food
    Store
White dextrine, C
White lead, H
White spirit (Turps substitute), H
Whiting, H
Witch hazel, C

Zinc, Metal merchant
Zinc chloride, C
Zinc oleate, C
Zinc oxide, C

INDEX

EDITORS' NOTE

In this second edition of *The Book of Practical Household Formulas* we have been able to include a number of useful additional formulas, largely due to readers' response to our invitation in the first edition to send us for consideration any formula they felt would be suitable for inclusion.

With the hope of expanding yet further in the third edition we are renewing our invitation, and our offer to pay £5 on publication to anyone whose formula we have included.

OWN FORMULAS

OWN FORMULAS

OWN FORMULAS